NEITHER FISH NOR FOWL

NEITHER FISH NOR FOWL

What Middle School Parents Need to Know in Today's Challenging World

Donna DeMarco

Archway Publishing books may be ordered through booksellers or by contacting:

Archway Publishing
1663 Liberty Drive
Bloomington, IN 47403
www.archwaypublishing.com
1 (888) 242-5904

Cover design and illustration by: Sherrie Longello

Introduction by: Gene DeMarco

ISBN: 978-1-4808-8103-7 (sc)
ISBN: 978-1-4808-8102-0 (e)

Library of Congress Control Number: 2019910363

Print information available on the last page.

Archway Publishing rev. date: 7/30/2019

In loving memory of my father, a man who changed people's lives for the better. You always believed in me and told me there wasn't anything I couldn't accomplish. Daddy, you are greatly missed, loved and thought of every day.

Dedication

This book is dedicated to my loving, supportive husband and partner, Gene, who has patiently stood by me during all the trials and tribulations that life, has brought our way. You have encouraged me to always reach for my dreams, hence the writing of this book. You have been my biggest supporter and always told me I'm the expert. This book would not have been written if it weren't for our wonderful, extraordinary children, Matt and Sara. You both gave me the strength, will and determination to fight cancer and become a survivor. You continue daily to bring joy, love and laughter to my life. When people ask me what my greatest life accomplishment has been, my response is my children who are caring, loving, amazing, successful adults. I deeply love all of you. You are the greatest gifts in my life.

Introduction

Being married to two teachers with a combined sixty-five plus years in the classroom, I feel particularly versed in the trials and tribulations of their profession. I've been privy to even the regrettable mistakes that honest teachers admit to. For example, the time a former teacher found live bullets in a seven year olds pocket. Not knowing what to do with the bullets, she kept them until the end of the day. Then gave them back to the student they came from. Although it was a different time then, it still seems obviously precarious. My point is that teachers make their share of faux pas. Some more serious than others, but it's our mistake to think they have all the answers.

I could go on with all the horror stories involving administrators, parents, and of course politically motivated officials, but for what purpose. You all have your share that make your guts churn or your face contort with disbelief.

No one knows your child better than you. While it's not the teacher's job to raise your child, this journey needs to be a collaborative effort between the teachers and parents.

Experience has always been the best teacher. And what we have here is an honest look at what to expect, and in most cases how to deal with the day-to-day difficulties in raising and guiding your middle school child toward high school and beyond.

Every child is different, and demands a unique assessment of their particulars. But in general this author pinpoints the stages, and challenges of each with a practical plan and additional resources to help you through it all. If you've ever felt that there is no place to turn, this guide will be a welcomed initiative, if you're willing to do your part.

PREFACE

Why Do They Drive Us Crazy?

An intended goal for me in writing this book is to share experiences, anecdotes, and helpful strategies for parents who are living with middle school children. At no time do I profess to be an expert, only an educator of thirty years who has encountered and taught over 6,000 students. College, graduate school, and professional development courses provide technical training but do not prepare an educator to make split-second decisions when dealing with students. A saying in my house when my children were growing up, when I either said the wrong thing, or handled a situation poorly, was they didn't teach that in mommy school and I would do better next time. I know you're thinking that response wouldn't last too long, but it really did work for years.

Sometimes we feel that we fail our children because we are not clear on the problem, we only have half the necessary information, or we are just exhausted and frustrated. No one expects you to be a perfect parent, but I have always felt that knowledge is power. So, let me impart my knowledge and help you to survive middle school with your children.

The most asked question, as a middle school reading

teacher was, how long does the answer have to be? The answer was, write enough to answer the question. The response was, I don't know what to write about. I always told my students and my children that the easiest thing to write about is your personal experience. I would tell them, you are the expert and your story is one that deserves to be told. As the words left my mouth the look of confusion and despair was written all over their faces. That's why I want to share with you the things I experienced and learned over the past thirty-plus years as an educator in public schools and adjunct college professor, as well as parenting two middle school aged children. I am pleased to report that the three of us survived and they are well-adjusted, professional adults in spite of the turmoil during their middle school years. There were days I would come home disheveled, depressed, and exhausted, and wondering how can twelve to fourteen year olds get to me this way. They do excel in knowing how to push your buttons.

Middle school students are too old for coddling, but too young to be left alone to their own devices. Where do they fit in, and how do they cope making decisions? Adolescence is known to be that extremely awkward stage of development where they are no longer children, but not quite mature adults. Therefore, I have described them as neither fish nor fowl. Boys at this age are growing out of their clothes more quickly than parents want to accept, while girls seem to want to wear skimpier clothing and appear at least five years older than their actual age. Experience has shown me they don't always make rational decisions since their brains are on hiatus while hormones drive their thoughts and actions.

This book will help guide you through the middle school experience, and hopefully create a stronger, healthier bond with your child. Remember, every age brings its own problems, concerns and issues as well as opportunities; however, the middle school years seem to present the most challenging time in a child's life and academic endeavors.

Contents

1

Transitioning to Middle School

Our lives are always changing and evolving, and if you are someone who doesn't welcome change, then any transition can be an upsetting event. All of us have experienced new situations that have caused apprehension and fear of the unknown. Remember that first day at a new job, having to make a presentation, or moving to another city or state? Well, the anxieties are magnified for a child graduating from elementary school and moving forward to middle school. There can be a number of things that your child may become anxious about in making this major change in their life. Past students, as well as my own children, shared their concerns about how big the middle school was compared to their elementary building or riding a bus with older children, or perhaps just finding their classes.

There may be additional anxiety with having to deal with more teachers, completing harder work, making new friends, learning how to adjust to changing classes, and opening a locker. There are possibly a host of other issues that are plaguing your child upon entering middle school.

When a student leaves elementary school, many think

that they're, "the top banana." They were in the oldest grade in the school, the younger students looked up to them, and they literally ran the building. Now, they are entering a new building, starting all over, and facing many challenges. They are also going to be dealing with different adult personalities from all their new teachers. That nurturing teacher, who treated them like their second mom or dad and spent the majority of the day with them, is now being replaced by a team of core teachers, as well as non-core teachers, such as: those teaching: gym, computer, home and careers, technology, foreign language, and health.

Part of how well they deal with this transition will be based on the preparation that you have done to enable your child to feel confident and excited about this new venture they are ready to embark upon.

The preparation is neither involved nor difficult. Throughout this book, you will read about how important communication is between you and your child as well as the school personnel and staff. You need to attend orientation programs and take visits to the school during the summer, to help your child find their classes. And be available to answer all your child's questions. Remember these concerns may be different for each child.

This book discusses ways you can help your child maneuver through the next three years as positively as possible. It also provides survival tips for both of you during this process. That is an important point to never lose sight of; a process is exactly what this transition is all about. Each year may bring different issues, concerns and problems.

You may be anxious for your child to begin their middle school experience. You may have your own concerns, but don't share them with your child. You need to be calm and not allow your concerns to frighten them even more. They have enough of their own fears, and at first, they may not even want to discuss them with you. They may want to work things out for themselves. They may have been told horror stories by older children and need time to adjust to their new environment. Just be patient. Your child will let you know when your help is needed.

As a parent, you need to always keep lines of communication with your child open and listen intently to your child's concerns without minimizing his or her feelings. This can help make middle school a positive experience for both of you.

2

Making Parent-Teacher Conferences Productive

Talking to your child's teacher should be a positive experience for all concerned. There are scheduled conferences during the school year, and you can always request a meeting with any of your child's teachers.

Most middle schools have a team configuration with four to six core (English, social studies, science, and math) teachers teaching the same group of students. The team structure may vary from school to school, but: the concept of how to teach the middle school child most effectively remains the same. Proponents of this strategy believe it creates a relationship-based support system. "In schools, strategies such as teaming or advisories may be used to build stronger and more understanding relationships between teachers and students. The general idea is that students will be better served and more effectively taught if teachers know students well and understand their distinct learning needs, interests, and aspirations." [1]

The Glossary of Education Reform Teaming is an effective system that allows teachers to address any social or emotional as well as academic needs. Teachers can discuss the best way to personalize a learning experience and, if needed, can make a schedule change very easily. The team meets on a regular basis to discuss student issues. So depending on the size of the school your child attends, there can be more than one team per grade.

Parent-teacher conferences are usually scheduled the first half of the school year. Middle schools schedule a fifteen-minute meeting in a round- robin setting. In other words, the core teachers meet in one room, and you, the parent, move from teacher to teacher. It can appear a bit intimidating, but this does not have to be the case. Non-core teachers, such as reading, language, health, home and careers, physical education, will probably be in different locations in the building. You can select which teachers you would like to speak with during parent conferences. Every school may have a different configuration for their conferences, but parents have the opportunity to meet all their children's teachers.

The most important aspect of the conference is your attendance. Selecting a meeting time, being punctual, and having an open mind are key elements to a successful conference. You also send a loud message that you are involved in your child's education, and you want a relationship with his or her teachers.

Parenttoolkit.com states that, "You should expect a less holistic view of your child than in elementary school." [2] Since middle school teachers spend less than an hour a day with your child, they usually focus on academic performance and classroom behavior.

The elementary teacher spent all day every day with your child and could comment on social development and peer interactions, as well as overall academic abilities. This doesn't mean that you should still not ask questions about social and emotional concerns, especially if you sense your child is having problems. Speaking to each teacher gives you a more complete picture of his or her day. There may be an issue in only one class, and you can address your concerns to that specific teacher and broach the subject with other teachers to gain a better perspective on the issue.

As a parent, it is important to prepare or do your homework before attending the parent-teacher conference. Here are a few helpful tips.

1. Speak to your child before attending the conference. Discuss with your child any issues they are having in a particular class. You probably have been told who their favorite or least favorite teacher is and why. Ask your child if there is anything they want you to discuss or ask the teacher.

2. Have prepared questions. Since time is limited, it is helpful to write down the questions that you want to ask. You can always set up another time to meet if you feel all your concerns were not addressed.

3. Keep an open mind during the conference. The teachers may be telling you a scenario that is different from what your child shared with you concerning a specific class.

4. Have a plan for communication going forward in the school year. It is important to let the teachers know the best way to communicate with you. Make sure they have the correct email address and phone numbers. You can request weekly or monthly progress reports. Let the teachers know that you want to be notified as soon as a problem arises.

5. Make sure you share personal information about medical issues, problems at home that could affect your child's learning, or any evidence of bullying. National Parent Teacher Association President, Betsy Landers, states that, "Many times your personal knowledge can be the key to helping your child to be more successful." [3]

Remember, a conference should be collaboration, not a confrontation. When it comes to our children we can be very defensive. We also don't appreciate another adult telling us that our "perfect" child is being the class clown or is falling asleep in class.

It may not be easy, but try not to verbally attack your child the moment you get home. Punishment has already begun while they are sitting home knowing their teachers may be giving their parents some upsetting news. They may be anticipating your wrath upon returning home. Try to calmly discuss key points and let them share their feelings and perceptions. I'm not saying this is easy, but we all respond better to not being yelled at or judged. Also, always start with something positive; this will get their attention and begin your conversation on a better tone.

Most of these scheduled conferences do not allow the time to get into very in-depth discussions. Before you leave, set up another time when you can discuss a specific issue, concern, or problem. The important thing to remember is both you and the teachers want your child to have a positive and rewarding school year where they are able to grow academically, emotionally and socially.

3

The Adolescent Brain

Just like everything else in a teenager's life, their brain is a work in progress. What that means exactly is that they are trying to figure out where they fit in. There are many changes going on during the middle school years. First let's look at their attitudes–and there's plenty of that to go around. It seems at times that their major goal in life is to push any adult's buttons. You look at your child or student and ask yourself what demon has taken over their minds today.

Some days your middle school child wants their independence, and other days they want to be babied. Sara Johnson, an assistant professor at the John Hopkins Bloomberg School of Public Health, tells us that, "the brain's most dramatic growth spurt occurs in adolescence." Sara Johnson also has identified 5 interesting facts about the teen brain. They are as follows:

1. New Thinking Skills

Due to the increase in brain matter, the teen brain becomes more interconnected and gains processing power. Adolescents start to have the computational and decision-making skills of an adult – if given time and access to information.

But in the heat of the moment, their decision-making can and will be overly influenced by emotions.

2. Intense Emotions

Puberty is the beginning of major changes in the limbic system, which refers to the part of the brain that not only helps regulate heart rate and blood sugar levels, but also is critical to the formation of memories and emotions.

Part of the limbic system is thought to connect sensory information to emotional responses.

Johnson also says that, "You can be as careful as possible and you will still have tears or anger at times because they have misunderstood what you have said."

3. Peer Pressure

As teens become better at thinking abstractly, their social anxiety increases, according to research in the Annals of the New York Academy of Sciences published in 2004.

Abstract reasoning makes it possible for a person to view oneself through the eyes of others.

For this reason, adolescents find the approval of their peers to be paramount.

Research also tells us, "Friends also provide teens with opportunities to learn skills such as negotiating, compromise and group planning."

4. Measuring Risk

While an adolescent's brain is developing, the changes may cause the teen to be more susceptible to engaging in irrational behaviors that may involve trying cigarettes, drugs, and getting into disagreements that may lead to fighting.

Taking risks are kids ways of understanding themselves in the world around them.

Adults in teens' lives need to be supportive in listening, answering questions, and helping them to arrive at solutions.

5. 'I am the Center of the Universe'

"The hormone changes at puberty have huge effects on the brain, one of which is to spur the production of more receptors for oxytocin," according to research detailed in a 2008 issue of the Journal Developmental Review.

Research indicates that this oxytocin, also described as the, "bonding hormone," has been connected with one feeling very self-conscious, and therefore a teen may be feeling like everyone is judging them.

Johnson states that, "It's the first time they are seeing themselves in the world, meaning greater autonomy has opened their eyes to what lies beyond their families and school." [4]

My all-time favorite expression that I heard in school was, "My bad." That was supposed to excuse everything that came before that wonderful statement of apology.

If we work with the premise that the only people who make sense in their lives are their friends, then we can all agree that in the hierarchy of people in their lives, parents, teachers and any adult rank at the bottom of the list. Middle school students are obsessed with what their friends think about them, and their moods are affected by the outcome of these relationships. To make matters worse these dynamics are constantly changing. You try to ask how things are going with their friend and you're given this look like you said something awful because they are not talking to that person anymore.

Friendships can be very short lived during the middle school years.

I'm not sure what the true definition of "dating," is but for a sixth through eighth grader, it's a moment during lunch when one person says to the other, "Do you want to be boyfriend and girlfriend?" Now, that doesn't mean they actually ever date or see each other outside of school. They have their own vocabulary, which can't be found in Webster's Dictionary. One lesson we try to instill in our children is to be a leader not a follower. How's that working for you? Being a single parent, I had no one to share these trying times with, except friends and other teachers. As the saying goes, "misery loves company." Talking to others helped with the idea that I wasn't doing anything wrong, because my once adorable loving children were now creatures that wanted nothing to do with me.

If you can remove yourself from the personal aspect and see that these young people have a brain but not one that is functioning properly, you can start to look at the situation from a different perspective. For example, I was once told that if your adolescent child tells you that they hate you on a regular basis, then you are doing a great job at parenting.

That's a hard thing to hear from your child but the reality of the situation is that you have to stand your ground no matter what verbal response might follow.

The pre-teen wants to be independent but finds that they need to be dependent to function. With no means of transportation, they require an adult to drive them as well as provide them with money for their social activities. However, they don't want any adult, especially a parent, to be within a bird's eye view of them. Once, I went to the mall with my son when he was in seventh grade. Upon entering the mall he told me that I could not walk next to him and asked if I could move to the other side. I think the look on my face made it quite clear to him that I was not obliging his request.

Adolescents can be extremely resourceful and creative when they want something. As part of the middle school English curriculum students are taught how to write a persuasive essay. The majority never really totally understood how to present their arguments and prove their thesis, so the example I would use is how to plead with your parents to get them to do something you want when you know their answer will be no. Teens are excellent at arguing a case for parents to get them to agree with their point of view. We as adults just feel worn down, so sometimes we tend to give in to their demands. It's just the easiest way at the time. I'm sure you understand what I'm talking about. If you don't, hopefully my examples will at least put a smile on your face.

Your child needs some help doing a science project and you are the one actually working on the experiment while they are watching television or on the computer. Or, you are taking care of the pet they promised that they would feed, walk, and take care of everything. My favorite is when you are exhausted and tell your child numerous times that you don't want to leave the house and then you find yourself either at the mall, taking them to a friend's house or going out to dinner while the food you planned on cooking is sitting on your counter at home.

Research has told us that our brains continue to change during our life span. So if we accept this premise that the adolescent's brain is definitely a work in progress, then we can start to delve into how to survive these wonderful formative years.

First, you need to be the adult in charge even if you feel that you are losing control. Remember when your child was going through the terrible twos and they acted like they were the center of everything? In order to understand this concept, Bloom's Taxonomy was created in 1956 under the leadership of educational psychologist, Dr. Benjamin Bloom, [5] in order to promote higher forms in thinking in education.

His findings showed us those higher levels of thinking such as reasoning and analyzing occur in later years of development. When talking about the adolescent brain you need to understand that it is not being used to its fullest potential. As your child matures in years so will the development of their brain.

Think of the depiction of the devil and an angel inside your child's mind. Now, the rational part of their thinking tells them what is right and on the other hand what is wrong. Knowing this does not make their decision easy because other factors come into play for them: Does selecting the inappropriate behavior make them look "cool" in the eyes of their friends? Is it worth possibly getting into trouble to fit in with the popular group of students? So, the decision to act in a way that they know is wrong can be justified if they are doing it for the right reasons. As parents and teachers we may view adolescents' choices as not being rational or right, but in their minds the means justify the end. A teenager may know that they will possibly be punished for going against their parents' explicit rules but once again in their mind, getting in trouble at home or school is worth it for the acceptance of their peers.

Adolescents do not want to acknowledge that they do not know what's going on, so they would rather lie than appear stupid in front of their friends or other adults. Their responses to posed questions do not make sense to us, while they know exactly what they are saying and why. There is a television commercial where a teenager cops an attitude toward his father while dealing with a flat tire. The father asks him if he knows what a lug wrench is and he responds to his father with an attitude, as if to say of course I know what a lug wrench looks like, but in reality he has no clue. He thinks he is proving to his father that he can handle the situation, when it is clear that the young man will not be able to change the flat tire.

The adolescent brain can be viewed as a short-circuited switchboard. The wiring is off. The real problem is how do we understand the thought process that an adolescent goes through in making decisions. Since there is little logical or analytical processing occurring during these developmental years there must be something else controlling decisions. This something else is hormones. Your child has raging hormones that seem to overpower the logical thought process.

So we need to understand that during the wonderful middle school years, your child is often not thinking or acting rationally. At times trying to have an intellectual conversation with them may really be an exercise in futility. Puberty has taken control over their mind and body.

Your adolescent child is behaving the way their minds and bodies are programmed at their age. An example of this is evident in an excerpt from the novel *The Great Alone* by Kristin Hannah, in which she depicts the life of a thirteen-year-old girl living in the 1970s in Alaska. The girl's father is driving her to the one-room schoolhouse and she tells him to stop before getting to the building. The father is disappointed when she says, "Can I walk from here?" The girl states that, "She was too nervous to smooth his ruffled feelings. One thing was true of every school she'd been at was this: once you hit junior high, parents were to be absent. The chances of them embarrassing you were sky-high." [6]

Regardless of the time period, this is normal behavior for the workings of an adolescent brain.

4

The Importance of Middle School Friendships

Friendships are important in every stage of life. Toddlers play independently alongside their friends. When we enter kindergarten our fears and uncertainties seem to melt away when we recognize a familiar face in the classroom. This comfortable feeling only seems to intensify as we get older and find ourselves in unfamiliar, threatening or just new situations.

As an adult, if we haven't had the necessity to move around, our friendships started developing at a very young age. Every new school year we hoped and prayed that certain friends would be in our class the following year. There is fear and disappointment when we are separated, but there is always that feeling of relief when we recognize a friend's face in a new situation. Our hope is that we will become better friends during the school year. This bond gives us the comfort that whatever happens we will go through it together, sharing the good and the bad.

Friends teach us to share our most precious possessions, ideas and ultimately fears, private thoughts and feelings. Remember a sleep over with your best friend where you stayed up all night talking, laughing, and possibly shedding some tears? Bonds of friendship can last a lifetime or can be a short-lived bond with someone passing through your life.

During elementary school one's group of friends may have been from your neighborhood, the ones you either walked to school with or sat next to on the bus. You always seemed to know the same kids throughout fifth grade. Most of your socializing was in groups or with a couple of friends riding bikes, going to each other's houses, and just enjoying being young children together.

You had one teacher who knew all your quirks and liked you and accepted you for who you were. Your parents still were your heroes and they made all the bad stuff in your life tolerable because you were "the fixer" for whatever came along.

Upon entering middle school, the one teacher is no longer there to be with you for six hours a day and is replaced by four subject teachers and at least three or four more non-core teachers with classes that may be every day or every other day for possibly half a year.

In middle school, your child's safety-net friend is replaced or gone altogether, and the dynamics of friendships have been greatly altered: one of many changes headed their way. Middle school is like no other time in your child's life and friendships are very important. Peer pressure is most prevalent during these years. The adolescent is dealing with so many changes in their lives and friendships are high on the list of priorities.

Your child's world is rocked, because all their friends have lunch a different period from theirs, or there is no one they know or like in gym class. Their world is shattered the very first day of school. Telling them they can make new friends is a foreign idea. Now what happens?

As parents and teachers we want the best possible school year for our children and students, but we can't always be there with them to encourage or help them develop new friendships. It is not part of our job description, and to tell you the truth they wouldn't listen to any adult. So your once happy-go-lucky elementary student is now an unhappy middle school child who hates school.

In Chapter 3 concerning the adolescent brain we know for a fact that a lot is going on developmentally, physically, and sexually. Also if you recall, when your child was young you planned the play dates and selected the activities, therefore controlling the children they played with and ultimately became friendly with during their preschool, primary and upper elementary years. Now, all that control is completely gone. At best, you are limited in controlling friend selection.

As a teacher, I would have parents come to a parent/teacher conference and ask who their child was hanging around with in school and make concerned comments about their child's new friends. As a parent you do have control over who comes to see your child at your home, who they go out with and what activities they attend. School is not part of your domain. Remember when your child came home and told you everything about their day, what every child brought for show and tell, as well as who shared their snack with them in the morning? Now when the question is posed, "How was your day," you get one-word answers like fine, okay, or nothing happened. All of a sudden your bubbly, happy, carefree child is nowhere to be found.

Not to worry! It's a temporary situation. In middle school

friendships are constantly changing. It's all about being accepted as part of a group. Your child is searching for friends they can feel comfortable with and just be themself.

Did you know that your child's friend is the smartest, most knowing person in the world? Well, they must be because what they say matters the most. You as a parent are now on the bottom of that ladder and you don't understand anything that matters, but their friends "get them."

Well, you're happy when they're happy and you're even relieved knowing they have friends, but there's a small problem because you're not quite pleased with their friend selection. First, your child has begun to metamorphose into a person you don't recognize any more. They changed their appearance, style of clothing, choice of words, and total demeanor. It could be one thing or all the above. What now? Second, your cheerful child has become moody and short with you, or even nasty.

In this time of change and growth, the adolescent is trying to find out who they are and what is important to them. For the first time in their lives they want to develop their own style, whether it is changing a hairstyle or hair color or dressing differently than they had during elementary school.

Upon entering middle school every morning the way they look is important as far as how they are perceived by others. I always felt that having a dress code in public schools would eliminate this element of stress and problems, not to mention expense, for the student who doesn't have the financial means to buy designer clothes or sneakers. It would also remove this element of competition among students. Unfortunately, the reality is that kids are made fun of because of what they are wearing on a certain day. Another consideration is your adolescent child wants a style of their own or just wants what their friend is wearing.

In middle school, my son chose a hairstyle for himself that wasn't unattractive; it's just that the cut was for straight hair and his definitely was not straight and could have been described as thick and wavy. Upon leaving the salon the ride home would always be rather quiet since he wasn't happy, but when I suggested a different style more conducive to his type of hair, I was the one who didn't understand and he liked the way it looked. Eventually, he did change the hairstyle but not before a few years of dissension between us.

Some of the female students I had in classes definitely looked different upon arriving at school than when they left the house. If I'm not making myself clear, a skirt was much shorter, a top was more fitted and make up was added to their beautiful face and complexion on their way to school.

Most of their moodiness has to do with their friends. At this age an adolescent's perception of himself or herself is seen through the eyes of their peers. If there is total acceptance, there is happiness in their daily lives, but if the dynamics of their peer group changes, there is unhappiness. In their minds as a parent you don't understand what they have to deal with on a daily basis. As adults, we know from first-hand experience that kids can be mean.

In today's society peer pressure seems to prevail more in a middle school student's life than years ago. Part of the problem is that kids are growing up much earlier and want to act and look older than their actual age. Life was much simpler when we were growing up. We played outside all day and only came home when it was time to eat or it got dark out. Today if a middle school child doesn't wear the accepted clothing, or isn't considered "cool" by their peers, that is a problem. The perception of their self worth is directly affected by their friends' comments or the way they are treated by the other students around them.

Parents and educators spend a lot of time building up their children and students' positive self-images. We try to focus on the individual and explain that they should be leaders not followers; but in reality they listen to the popular student and want to be recognized as being associated with that particular person or group.

Therefore, the tendency is to follow the leader and possibly go against what they truly know and believe even though it is opposite to the way they were brought up to think or behave.

So what can we do? Definitely not judge them or tell them they need to look for other friends, unless you want to close whatever minimal window they have kept open to be part of their social world. It's not easy to stand by and watch a snowball roll down a hill as it rapidly picks up momentum and strength, but what can you do to stay out of its path of destruction? You can include yourself in your child's social life without letting them know you are looking out for their best interest. For example, offer to drop off or pick up from a weekend event. This way you can actually meet the friends they are spending time with in and out of school. You can suggest your child invite friends to your house, giving them the space to have their time alone but still supervising the event.

If your child doesn't want you to ever meet the kids they are spending time with, a red flag should go up. Try to find out why. If your child wants to stay over a friend's house and you haven't met them or are unsure you want your child to be associating with them, suggest having them over for dinner prior to the sleepover and just say it's your way of reciprocating for their kindness. Suggest to at least talking to their friends' parent. Preteens can be very secretive and manipulative to make adults feel uneasy. Didn't you ever tell your parent you were going one place and knew you had other plans and had no intention of letting them know?

Life today is so much more complicated, dangerous and fast paced than when we were growing up. We can track our children's phones and monitor their Internet access but they have their own codes and secret language to keep parents unclear of their intentions. I'm not implying that your child is being deceitful on purpose; it's just them slowly pulling away from total dependence and trying to take control over their own choices. With these choices, however, there are consequences for actions that go against your implicit rules. As a parent you should have complete control over your child's impulsive actions.

Parents used to ask me who their child's choice of friends were at school because they were concerned since their child's grades had slipped, or they were acting differently than they usually acted, or they saw changes in their child's overall demeanor that concerned them. I would respond by asking them if they wanted me to talk to them as their child's teacher or as a parent. The response was usually as a parent, asking how I would handle the same situation.

It would always boggle my mind when an honor student selected the athletic student who was on academic probation to be their boyfriend/girlfriend.

Sometimes middle school kids act in a certain way to get a reaction or seek attention. Perhaps, they may choose to be with someone knowing their parent would not approve of their decision.

As a parent you want to allow your child a certain amount of freedom once they enter middle school, but with that freedom comes responsibility. I used to say, "Let your child have the freedom but hold on tight to the reins and pull them in when needed."

In the past a child wanted to emulate the brightest student, but now that is not necessarily the case. The primary concern of a parent is their child's health and well-being. Therefore, one may overly react to a poor decision about a friendship made by their child.

I'm not advocating that you allow your child to make decisions about friends that may have a negative effect in their lives, but at the same time you need to listen to what they have to say and try to find a compromise. You can encourage them to get involved in extracurricular activities that may broaden their circle of friends. For example sports, clubs, honor society. You can also try community involvement where you as a parent can work alongside your child. Your adolescent, however, needs to feel that these are ultimately their decisions. There is nothing worse than forcing a preteen or teenager to attend functions that they have no interest in. You know the old adage that, "You can lead a horse to water but you can't make it drink."

In summary, middle school friendships can be short lived or can end up being your child's best friends for life. The most important thing to consider is how do these friendships affect your child's life. Are these other kids a negative or positive influence? You do know that ultimately your child is going to talk to and possibly look up to a classmate who in your opinion is not someone who has a positive influence. You need to take comfort in the fact that you are being the best parent you can be and that you have and will continue to raise your child according to your values. Remember most of all, that friends may come and go but family will always be there for guidance, support and love. Our role is not to judge our children's selections of friends but to be available to help them work through these decisions so they are happy and enjoy their middle school experiences without feeling any sense of ostracism or little self worth. Your child's peers are the center of their universe during the middle school years.

5

Specific Concerns and Issues
in Middle School

There are two ways to address this topic. One is from your child's perspective and the other is from the parent's. There are common concerns that middle school children experience. Since 9/11 our lives have changed; schools are no longer the safe havens they used to be and young people are feeling more anxiety in their lives. Children have experienced anxious situations even before understanding the meaning of the word. With that being said, I'm sure we can agree that life is different for our children than when we were in school. Middle school students encounter a lot of pressure in their daily life. Try to understand their dilemmas and be supportive by helping them to solve their problems.

If I were to ask both you and your middle school student to list their concerns about attending middle school, the lists may be totally different or some issues might overlap. During my experience teaching adolescents, attending special education meetings, participating in professional developmental workshops, I have spent my years learning about issues specific to middle school students and strategies to help them deal with these important life-altering issues. The following list is not in any order of importance since they are all important to the child that is dealing with them. Just remember each age brings its own problems, concerns and obstacles.

Bullying

Every school has a "no bullying" tolerance. Administrators and teachers have developed programs and assemblies where students are taught that bullying is wrong, and not condoned in their school.

Unfortunately, bullies have always existed and probably always will. It is the teacher's responsibility to report any evidence of bullying. I have intervened in bullying situations and I was unable to do anything because the student being bullied denied that anything was going on for fear of retribution from other students. The problem is incidents occur when an adult is not in earshot, or before or after school, in a locker room or in a bathroom. In today's society we are dealing with cyber bullying and that is a nationwide problem. It is not my place to tell you that you should be monitoring your child's computer history but you need to be informed about who they are texting and emailing. We know our middle school child does not confide in us, so we need to be extremely vigilant in looking for any negative changes in your child's demeanor. If you suspect that your child is being bullied, try to talk to them and get as much information as you can and definitely contact the school immediately. The sooner you become aware of the situation and bring it to the attention of the authorities the sooner the problem can be rectified.

Academics

Doing well academically in middle school will usually be more of a parent's concern than their child's. We are very pleased and proud that our child has made the high honor or honor roll, but is it as important to them? For many years, I was the advisor for the National Junior Honor Society and every year I would receive calls from parents who wanted their child to be inducted even though their GPA (grade point average) was lower than the mandatory average. Sometimes kids felt pressure from their parents to attain a certain grade and they would rebel by not completing assignments and purposely doing poorly. I can't tell you how many kids know exactly how many points they need to pass, or how long they can get away without doing homework, or know they can fail a course or two and still be passed to the next grade. I've experienced bright students acting less bright so their friends will accept them. Some students are self-motivated to want to excel and care about their grades while others are less concerned and enjoy the social aspect of middle school.

Where does the pressure come from? I recall being very excited to tell my father that I scored 99 on a test and his response was, "Why didn't you get a 100?" Obviously, it was not the response I was hoping for at the time but it did make me wonder if I needed to get a perfect score all the time. The approach I used with my own children was to ask them if they felt they did the best they could on a test. In other words, had they studied the correct material, put in an appropriate amount of time preparing for a test or an assignment, and were they pleased with the outcome. Sometimes kids are harder on themselves than their parents are on them.

Be careful though, in case you don't get the response you were hoping to hear. What does it mean when you are asked if your child is doing well in school? Is your child being compared to a brighter sibling or other students in their class? When it comes to academics children should only be competing with themselves.

How do we motivate our children to want to do well? Parents have been known to use bribery with money or gifts for attaining a certain grade. I know this because my children would tell me that their friends were given money for an A grade on their report card. They were not happy when I explained to them that going to school was their job and that I was not paying them anything to do their expected job. As you probably can surmise this did not go over too well in our home. So, I explained that they should want to do well for themselves and for their future.

Only a few years in school can lead to a lifetime of successful and good living. During high school, students get a ranking based on their GPA but in middle school kids will tell you that their grades don't matter. Your response can be that their academic performance in middle school will affect their high school classes. Bribery may work for a short period of time but kids always expect and want more while doing less and you really don't want to go down that road.

During the primary years, kindergarten to fifth grade, children are spoon-fed information and usually have one main teacher that they spend the majority of their day with in school. This teacher controls the class work as well as assigned projects and homework. The classroom teacher has an excellent understanding of how your child learns, participates in the classroom and works independently and within a group setting. This primary teacher is the adult you contact with any questions, concerns or suggestions.

Upon entering middle school as stated in Chapter 1, the structure for your child's education changes. Instead of one teacher there is now a team or group of teachers instructing your child. For some children this change is overwhelming and perhaps confusing, and may affect their learning.

Children tend to excel academically in those classes where they like the teacher and subject matter. When your middle school student tells you that their grades don't count until they get to high school, that statement does have some validity; however, it's not the whole story. Their grades may not count towards high school or college but they do matter in other ways. In an article from Get Schooled it states that, "Students' middle school grades are a crucial point of intervention. Students show considerable growth and declines between fifth and eighth grade. Students need very high grades to be on course to earn high grades in high school. In fact, only those students who leave eighth grade with GPAs of at least 3.0 have even a moderate chance of earning a GPA of 3.0 in high school, the threshold for being considered college-bound." [7]

Middle school students, like any other students, need to take pride in themselves and their grades. Their performance will directly affect the classes they are scheduled to be in for the next three years. Most content area classes are scheduled by homogeneous grouping, which means students with the same academic ability are grouped together. Some middle schools have regent, honor and advanced classes where the prerequisite is the student's course grade or overall GPA for the previous year. So, regardless of what your child says middle school grades do matter.

Dr. Robert Balkans, a noted researcher from John Hopkins University states that, "The middle school years may be the most important years in a child's education, the most fertile years. It is during this time that students ask and answer the question for themselves. Is schooling for me?" [8]

Middle school doesn't always bring out the best in all children. By that I mean, as they begin to enter adolescence and gain more independence they may for the first time start having behavioral issues, not wanting to attend school, and start getting low grades in classes that they had done well, in elementary school. By every measure, academics in middle school are crucial for your child's educational career.

Most schools provide progress reports, which are generated halfway through the quarter. There are usually four quarters in a school year. As much as your middle school child is maturing and wanting to be independent, when it comes to their grades, you really need to know how they are performing. You may get a different response from your child and their teacher concerning their grade. Some schools have a portal where all grades as well as missing assignments are listed and you can find out a particular grade at any time. It is better to have a clear understanding of your child's academic performance while there is plenty of time to make up work, do extra credit, or provide extra help if required.

Test Anxiety

Test anxiety [9] has become a prominent issue in middle school. Some students become paralyzed over taking teacher prepared or standardized tests. They may become physically as well as emotionally ill. Students suffering with test anxiety have attendance issues, which leads to less time in the classroom causing gaps in learning important material. I do believe this is a serious condition, especially to the child experiencing high anxiety.

As a parent, you will be able to recognize the symptoms and signs. If your child appears to be excessively worried or stressed about school, try to talk about what they are feeling.

The three main causes of test performance anxiety are fear of failure, lack of preparation and poor test history. Your child may exhibit physical symptoms, such as: headaches, nausea and diarrhea, racing heart rate or shortness of breath. These symptoms could cause a panic attack.

Along with physical signs there can also be emotional signs of test anxiety. It's not uncommon for an adolescent to act out, but in these circumstances the emotional responses could be feelings of anger, a sense of helplessness or severe disappointment. There can also be evidence of behavioral symptoms such as difficulty with concentration and negative thoughts.

There are several ways you can help your child at home with test anxiety. Teaching your child to be prepared can lower anxiety. Help them break a big assignment or test preparation into smaller tasks. There are many strategies that can be used to help with test taking.

You need to explain that reading directions and breaking them down in parts is crucial, as well as reading the whole question. Always reinforce positive results. Being negative does not accomplish anything other than cause more anxiety.

Staying focused is a skill that needs to be developed.

Middle school students, as a whole, are easily distracted. There is nothing worse than looking over at a friend who appears to be handling the test easily while you are stuck on questions. Creating a system of methodically answering questions can help develop a sense of confidence. Have your child try to practice relaxation techniques. This can be accomplished with parental or professional guidance. Lastly, keeping your child healthy by getting a good night's rest, eating healthy and learning how to cope with stress will help your child handle life's problems.

Interpersonal Relationships

Middle school is a time of new experiences and opportunities. There are clubs, sports, dances, trips, and meeting new friends from different schools. Some adolescents have no problem with social interactions while others are uncomfortable in new situations. There is also the added pressure of talking with the opposite sex as well as dating. We like to think that our child will handle situations without any support from their parents but that is unrealistic. Even adults are not always comfortable in all settings. As you know, adolescents mature at different rates, so it is necessary to know how your child is adapting in these new situations and be available to answer questions and possibly give suggestions in dealing with other students and adults.

Home Dynamics

Family structures today are different from when we were children. It is not uncommon for kids to live with their grandparents, aunts or uncles, or two moms or two dads. Today's children are dealing with divorces, sick parents and possibly the loss of one. When I was in middle school my best friend's mother had cancer. None of our friends knew what that was and had no understanding of what Natalie was dealing with in taking care of her mom. What I remember most was how much she grew up and how sad she was most of the time. Cancer is an illness that not only affects the person that is stricken with the condition. It permeates the entire family. Sometimes, children of sick parents are left out of discussions, treatments, and they are confused and possibly scared. The other parent is over stressed and may not have the time or strength to be there for their children. Make sure you contact the school and let them know the situation so professionals can help your child. Cancer is not the only condition that families have to deal with on a daily basis. Any health situation will have a direct effect upon children. Every home dynamic is different, but the one defining factor is that children need loving, supportive, caring adults in their lives.

Self Image

I think everyone can relate to a time in their life when they were a bit envious or downright jealous of another person. This feeling may have only been a fleeting moment or maybe lasted for years. We may look at certain people during our life and think they seem to have it all: possibly good looks, athletic ability, money or just an easier life than we are experiencing. The average person understands the expression: "the grass is always greener on the other side," and realizes that just because something appears one way it doesn't necessarily mean that's the way it actually is in life. For an adolescent child who may feel awkward because they're a little socially inept or their body is growing at an exceedingly fast rate or just the opposite and all their friends are changing physically and they're not, can result in a difficult time where some kids are experiencing a poor self image. Remember, middle school kids are not thinking rationally about things in general. Their raging hormones have taken over their sense of reasoning. So we need to constantly reassure them that their acne will not last forever, their braces will come off their teeth, they are not the only ones wearing glasses, or they will not always be the shortest one in the class. During this time parents need to remind their child about their strengths and other positive abilities, such as musical talents, artistic abilities, or just the fact they are a great kid. This is a good time to get them involved in volunteering and possibly meeting other kids outside of school where there is not so much competition.

I tell the story of my son, who asked why he had to do anything outside of school and I told him that not only did he need to give back to his community, but also he would have nothing to fill in on college applications. Boy, did he admit I was right about that one. If you see your child getting depressed or not sleeping or eating, make sure you speak to their doctor or other professionals. Hopefully once middle school is over, your child will begin to see itself in a most positive light.

Addictive Drugs Including Alcohol and Cigarettes

Middle school for some is definitely a time of wanting to fit in and possibly experiment with drugs or alcohol. When you were growing up, did you know of any kids who took pills out of their parents' medicine chest and brought them to a party? I didn't. That occurs today in our society. Would you ever think of standing outside a liquor store and paying someone to buy you beer? Kids do today. Do you remember the first time you tried a cigarette? We all do, and you probably didn't inhale it and if you did you still remember choking and not being able to stop coughing. No one expects our children to be perfect or never disappoint us, but the reality is, all these things and more are available to middle school children. We do have control when our kids are home with us, but there are a lot of hours when your child is not at home. I could spend hours just talking about peer pressure, but a parent is really at a disadvantage here. Your child may act differently when they're with their friends and feel pressured to do or try something they know is not a good idea. So, why do they drink a beer or smoke a cigarette or even try an illegal drug? Why did you do it? The simple response is their friends were doing it and they wanted to be accepted.

Once again being open and honest with your child is very important. Share some of your experiences so they understand that you really get what they're going through in trying to survive in today's society. Remember, being accepted among their peers is very important to them and you can help them to find their place without getting into habits that will be detrimental to their health, safety and well being.

6

Students With Special Needs

Any student who requires additional services or support is classified through the Special Education Department within your school. State law mandates that the student have an IEP or an Individual Educational Plan. This plan specifies the services your child is entitled to receive through the school district. When your child was in elementary school the responsibility for this plan rested primarily with the teacher. In middle school, your child attends various classes and every teacher is responsible for knowing what your child's disability is as well as what services they are entitled to for the school year. As I mentioned in the beginning of the book, I have taught at least 6,000 students during my career. Within one school year, I had at least one hundred students with IEPs. As the only adult in the room, I was expected to have all the information memorized and was responsible for making sure every student received his or her accommodations. With thirty students in a room, I was supposed to copy notes for one child, while reading questions to another and making sure that I provided extended time for the students that had that accommodation for test taking, as well as making sure the remainder of the students' needs were addressed.

Additionally, there were students who didn't want to be singled out and therefore denied their service. No one wants to be different in middle school even if it means his or her academics suffer.

What does special needs really mean? It is a very broad term but simply stated, any child who requires additional support or services outside of their regular education classroom has special needs. There is a wide range of accommodations once a student is classified as a special needs student. During the elementary years, most of the responsibility rests with the teacher in making sure the student receives the appropriate services that are specified in a child's IEP. However, if the student is in a "pull out program" (leaves the class for services), the other students are well aware that that person is being taken out of the room for a specific reason.

When it comes to reading groups, kids are well aware from day one the hierarchy of the reading groups regardless of the name of that group. It could be an animal name, a color or just a symbol, and the slow readers already are identified as needing extra help. Is this a bad thing? Not at all, it's just that kids are very perceptive about their surroundings and what other kids are doing.

The problem arises if students become identified as "different" since they require additional help or support. I don't need to state that kids at any age can be mean and tease other kids. So, over the years the child with special needs does not want to be singled out in any way and definitely doesn't want others to know they have extended time to complete assignments or tests, or have another adult read to them in front of their peers. The service must be offered but the student can refuse it.

Upon entering middle school, kids are scrutinized even more by their peers, so the realization that they don't want these services to be known by others becomes more prevalent.

What does it mean to have a child with special needs? All of our children require help and support but a special needs child requires additional services to enable them to be successful in school.

When students of mine would get frustrated or down on themselves because they weren't doing well in a class, I would always explain to them that we all need help at one time or another. In raising my own children, I had to explain everyone wants to be successful especially when they put the time and effort in to preparing for an assignment or test. Unfortunately, the desired outcome is not always attained. I spent a lot of time with my students building up their confidence and explaining that it's okay to receive help and direction when they are struggling.

Also, I think we can all agree that no one wants to admit they need help or support. Schools have a special education team to help students understand the importance of these accommodations and how teachers can help their child in receiving them.

Parents need to know and understand what services their child is receiving. There are ramifications if these services are not provided.

Any parent of a special needs child should be completely aware of what their child's special education classification means and receive documentation of all testing as well as reports written about their child. You need to be actively involved and attend all meetings as well as ask for a meeting if you feel that services are not being carried out properly. You can always ask for a parent advocate who will attend meetings with you, who can ask questions on your child's behalf as well as be there to support you. This advocate is also there so you never feel alone in fighting for services for your child. As I always told my students, there are no stupid questions so ask for clarification on any information you don't understand.

District educators attend numerous meetings a day. For you the only meeting that matters is the one for your child. You must play an integral part in your child's education. Once the accommodations are agreed upon, first question when the next meeting will be scheduled to determine if the services are working. Second, find out who your contact person is in the district if you have questions or concerns about the services. Third, ask what needs to be done to change the accommodations or reduce or eliminate them completely. No one knows your child better than you do and how they will react in certain situations, so feel free to add your input at these meetings. For some parents this process has been occurring since their child entered public school; for others, it may happen at the middle school level. Remember you are in the driver's seat, not the district.

Middle school brings its own problems and anxiety to kids, so compound this with being singled out as needing extra help and your child starts not liking school as much as they did before.

Districts are always trying to improve their instructions and programs, so in the late eighties inclusion classes were implemented. If you're not familiar with this concept, an inclusion class mixed regular education students with ten to twelve special education students, a regular education teacher, a special education teacher, and a special education assistant. The teachers collaborated and taught together. The special education teacher was responsible for the special education students' learning of material and would help them if there were any issues in understanding classwork, homework, taking notes or completing assignments. Additionally, they would monitor the students' progress and make sure they received their accommodations.

As a fourth grader my son was chosen to be in an inclusion class and, not being clear as to how this class was run, I had many questions. I recall asking the teacher what role was my child to have in this class. She told me that my son as a regular education student would be explaining things to other students and would be expected to work independently and be a self-starter. I asked her if she had met my son, because explaining things to others would involve him talking in class, which he never did unless specifically asked a direct question, and being a self-starter was not an attribute of my son. He would do the work that was asked of him but he would not explore things on his own. He felt very uncomfortable if he needed to be the center of attention and with that being said, he had a very tough year. To date, inclusive classrooms are part of educational programs in several states. However, if your child is singled out in middle school for being different, they may rebel and not accept the services they are supposed to receive as part of their accommodations.

Part of the responsibility rests with the teacher and the way they assist your child. No one else in the room should be aware of these services. The teacher can quietly talk to the student and explain what the accommodations are and it shouldn't have to be discussed during every class. Additionally, arrangements should be made ahead of time if the student will be completing a test in another room (usually the resource room). If your child comes home and is upset in any way concerning their accommodations feel free to contact the teacher. Remember, there is a chain of command for making a complaint. If you are not satisfied with the teacher's response there is the principal, director of the special education department and ultimately the superintendent. Your child's mental well-being is most important.

At home, you can support your child by reinforcing that these services are meant to make things easier for them and these services are rendered just to get them to the point where they can handle their academic school work by themselves. You can reinforce the fact that these accommodations will be reviewed, revised and possibility be eliminated completely. You can also encourage your child to speak to their teacher if these accommodations are stressing them in any way. Accommodations are put in place to help support and provide your child with the best academic environment possible.

There are definitely ramifications if any student's IEPs are not followed to the letter. As I stated earlier, make sure you have a signed copy so you know exactly the accommodations that have been created for your child. There are numerous websites that provide information on the rights of parents who have a special education child. You need to check with your state and familiarize yourself with the rules and regulations. Remember, information is power and when it comes to our children's well being we need to be armed with a lot of information. The district is liable if any of your child's teachers are not aware of the services.

As a parent we would do anything to protect our children and guaranteeing that their needs come first is our job. Being proactive when it comes to overseeing their academic needs is primary. If you notice any changes in your child's personality or behavior, act on it immediately. Sometimes there is a simple solution to a problem before it has time to escalate. Asking questions and taking an active role by communicating with both your child and their teachers will help to secure a positive learning environment.

Meditation

As parents and educators we want to enrich our children and students' lives. We need to find ways to sharpen and improve our strategies in helping adolescents. There is a lot of research on the Internet concerning the benefits of meditation. Today's society has changed dramatically since we went to school. Adolescents today are dealing with stressful events in their lives; competitive situations whether in sports or academics, test anxiety, as well as personal issues at home. There is scientific evidence that indicates meditation can benefit children's brains and behavior.

Meditation teaches us to focus on the present, and this concept has been proven to help children in their daily life. Studies show there has been greater success with meditation for adults but there are areas where children have benefited. An area where parents and teachers are concerned about with adolescents, especially those with special needs, is increased attention in school, attending to tasks, including completing assignments and studying. According to Forbes Pharmacy and Healthcare, "One 2004 study found that children with

ADHD who learned meditation with their parents twice weekly in a clinic setting, and kept practicing at home, had better concentration at home, and had better concentration at school, among other benefits.

Like adults, adolescents too must deal with stressful situations. Sometimes that stress is external while other times it is definitely internal. Most parents and teachers find it difficult to get adolescents to open up about what is going on in their lives let alone share what's bothering them. We need to find an avenue to allow adolescents to express themselves without any repercussions. Studies have shown, especially with kids that struggle academically, and those who have special needs when it comes to learning, have benefited from meditation and mindfulness exercises with a qualified expert. There has been evidence of improved mental health in turn promoting better attendance and ultimately more success in school.

The more a person is in tune with their own self-awareness, the more control they have over their choices and ultimate decision-making.

7

The Gifted Child

I am not sure if I can give you an exact definition, if you want to know what it means to have a gifted child. The agreed consensus is that, "children are gifted when their ability is significantly above the norm for their age." Giftedness may manifest in one or more domains such as intellectual, creative artistic, leadership, or in a specific academic field such as language arts, mathematics, or science." [10] Personally, I feel all children have special gifts and some walk, talk, or are proficient at a sport way beyond their years. Other children can sing, dance, act, or play an instrument because they are encouraged to perform. The definition for exceptional talent is," the ability to perform a skill at a level usually not reached until later years, perhaps as late as adulthood." Testing is part of every school district whether it is by a teacher, school psychologist or a state mandated exam; however the measures used for giftedness are IQ and achievement tests. There is more than one IQ test that can be utilized but the range is as follows:

115-129 mildly gifted
130-144 moderately gifted

145-159 highly gifted
160-170 exceptionally gifted
180 profoundly gifted

"These ranges are based on a standard bell curve which is a graph where the distribution is bell shaped which tapers away at each end. Most people fall in the range between 85 and 115 with 100 the absolute norm. This range is considered normal. The farther away from the absolute norm of 100 a child is, the greater the need for special educational accommodations, regardless of whether the distance is on the left or right of 100." [11]

I'm sure by the time your child has entered middle school, as a parent, you are aware if there is evidence of giftedness. Not every student enjoys school or has a fascination for learning but those who do tend to be high achievers. Some adolescents may not do well in their core subjects but excel on achievement tests. The motivation to learn comes from within the student but can definitely be fostered by parents and teachers. Gifted children tend to learn quickly and easily which leads to great success, and we know that nothing breeds success more than being successful.

I have always believed that motivation and success also comes from interest. The challenge of a problem, team activity or posed question can promote motivation within a person. Gifted adolescents usually possess a good memory, which enables learning to occur more easily.

Once your child has been identified as gifted there are decisions to be made. The first issue is, does the school your child attends have the appropriate gifted programs? Does your child want to attend any of these provided services? There is also the issue of whether your child's school district has to make other accommodations such as busing to other schools, and fitting this program into your child's schedule. Does your child need to extend their school day to attend gifted classes?

As stated in Chapter 6, on students with special needs, gifted adolescents may not want to be singled out for their abilities. Kids are merciless when it comes to students who are different during the middle school years.

As the parent, you need to have a clear understanding of the gifted area or areas in which your child has been identified as being a high achiever.

Your child may welcome the fact that they exhibit special talents and academic abilities. If they do, they will continue to flourish and experience exciting opportunities.

On the other hand, they may be resistant to attending additional classes, changing classes, missing out in subjects they previously enjoyed, or being separated from their friends. We can never lose sight of the fact that middle school kids' friends are the center of their universe, so changes in their lives may affect them in negative ways.

So, what are ways we can help these gifted children to embrace their special talents? As parents, once again you need to be actively involved in your child's schedule. Make sure that your child does not feel like they are sacrificing one course for another or taking a gifted class and losing their class of choice. Have the schoolwork with you. If possible, have your child be part of the planning of any gifted classes. Encourage them to keep an open mind and possibly audit or sit in a section of a gifted class or program. The object is to enhance their academic schedule, not make them feel like they are being punished for being bright.

As parents you want your child to attain their fullest potential but not at the risk of them feeling alienated or upset that they never get to see their friends because they are in a different building or have an extended day due to extra classes.

8

Should Your Child's Schoolwork Be Your Responsibility?

Personally, I do not see any value in Science Fairs or elaborate project assignments. If you have lived through your child preparing for a Science Fair project you understand what I am talking about.

The first hurdle is to get your child excited about participating in it. Some middle schools require all students to enter while others do not make it mandatory.

Not being very strong in the science field I had limited expertise to pass on project ideas to my children, so off we went to Barnes and Noble to sit and read books about other projects to share to try to excite them. Well, excite was never a word I could really use, and in all honesty I was never able to enthrall them on any plan of action. Additionally, I spent my Saturday afternoon really doing their work. Yes, it was my choice, but I felt I needed to support them in their endeavor and of course I wanted them to have a good project. We usually went for the comparing cereals and which one got soggy first, or which bubble gum made the biggest bubbles, or interviewing people on a certain topic and charting their results. It was always fun to come up with a hypothesis. Once a topic was chosen and a course of action was planned, there was the "stand up board" to be displayed at the fair. You know the project posters with three sections. There were tears and temper tantrums but we had projects to present. My daughter would always underestimate the time she needed to complete her assignments and would procrastinate in actually starting the project. When she went to bed I was still gluing pictures and charts to the board, printing letters and adding final touches.

The fun part for me was attending the science fair and being able to figure out the profession of the parent whose child had the most elaborate projects. Of course, they could explain how it was made, what its purpose was, and how long it took to complete the masterpiece. I'm not so sure their child had any understanding of the working of their project. They usually got first through third place and my children maybe got an honorable mention because they showed up. The next day the cardboard display was in the garbage.

I used to stress about how to get these projects done. I remember my son had to make a cell using only edible items, while my daughter had created numerous shoebox dioramas, and projects involving making Play Doh® and papier-mâché. Were any of these projects fun, I guess so. We spent quality time together and possibly learned something, but my kids could not accomplish these assignments without my assistance. It could have been just buying the necessary materials, heating up the materials or just cleaning up the mess.

I understand hands-on learning is wonderful but as a parent we need to step back and allow our children to do these projects by themselves as much as possible.

Every parent wants their child to be successful but what are the real purposes of these projects? As a teacher, I chose not to assign any project where money had to be spent to complete it. Additionally, I chose to have group projects and the students worked on them during class time.

Homework assignments have also become parents' responsibilities. Sometimes the parent has difficulty understanding the assigned activity. I learned about a wonderful site called Kahn Academy. There are thousands of topics where you are personally tutored on a specific topic. This website became my salvation. Again, not being very strong in math or science, I would call upon my teacher friends for assistance in completing my children's class work or homework assignments. Now you can say I may have enabled my children by doing this but do you really want your child to go to school without completing their work because they needed help?

The question I am trying to get across is how responsible should a parent be for their child's schoolwork? I don't feel there is a simple answer to how much you want to help or actually do your child's assignments but you always have to keep in mind it is their responsibility. Additionally, if you are spending a lot of time working on your child's projects or homework, I would definitely contact the teacher who assigned the work and discuss your feelings and or frustration. The class may be an honors class and too difficult for your child or your child may figure if they throw themself enough you will do their work.

In elementary school there is one teacher assigning homework and projects. In middle school all content area teachers have a lot of information to cover in a limited amount of time so extra reading, answering questions and doing research may be assigned for homework. The problem is that three teachers can assign a lot of homework on the same night. This can cause stress for your child. Add to their workload a full day of school, possibly sports, clubs or after school activities, so there's limited time to complete all their work. You as their parent want to help them and minimize their anxiety.

Adolescents want to stay up later and then have a difficult time getting up for school. I can't begin to tell you how many kids fall asleep in school. You can help your child by making sure they keep their work organized, explain the importance of time management and be there to answer questions and help them to locate information, but require them do the work.

Middle school has so many challenges for our children and figuring out what your role is, may not be easy. Remember your child is still dependent upon your guidance and support even when they think they can handle every situation that comes their way. Balancing their schoolwork, friends, and extracurricular activities can be overwhelming, so we need to help them organize these activities including their academic responsibilities. Only you can decide how responsible you want to be for any aspect of their life but just as you are expected to complete assignments at work, your child is expected to complete their assignments at school and home.

9

What Drives Teachers Crazy?

Wouldn't it be great if life came with a manual that told us the Do's and Don'ts for every situation? This way we would know ahead of time how to handle whatever life threw our way. Dealing with your child's teachers doesn't have such a manual, so having as much information as possible to cultivate a positive working relationship is the goal, which benefits everyone.

Think of your child's teacher like your pediatrician. By that I mean when you take your child to the doctor you don't diagnose their illness; that is the doctor's job. Don't get me wrong, you may have some good ideas to what is brewing inside your child's body because you have observed certain signs, such as a fever, loss of appetite, sore throat etc. However, sometimes the symptoms aren't always observable even through you know your child is not feeling well.

In receiving information about your child from a teacher don't ignore it and then when a situation gets worse claim you didn't know this or that was going on. Teachers, like other professionals, are trained to identify problems with their students whether it is academically, emotionally or physically.

Remember your child is no longer with one teacher for six hours a day. So, it is important not to ignore anytime a teacher reaches out and says they have concerns about your child. A teacher will always work hard to help your child, and having the support of parents benefits everyone.

I'm sure we will agree that you know your child best, but remember middle school children act differently away from their parents when they're with their peers. No matter how busy you are, so is the teacher. They have families, commitments and a life outside of school, and they are making your child's situation a main priority.

If you provide your own transportation for your child to and from school and a teacher seeks you out to speak with you about your child, get off your cell phone. There is nothing ruder than having a conversation while a teacher is attempting to communicate with information pertaining to your child. Remember, working together is the goal.

Either in the summer or the beginning of school, teachers provide a list of necessary supplies that will be needed for a student to be successful in their class. As a parent it is your responsibility to provide your child with these necessary items even if you think they are unnecessary or ridiculous. Believe it or not, thought and experiences have been used to identify the necessary supplies. It is always greatly appreciated by the teacher for each student to have the requested supplies on time. I don't think you would go to work without your necessary equipment such as a computer; phone, spreadsheets or whatever is necessary to perform your job. So when a parent is lackadaisical about providing their child with the necessary items, it drives teachers crazy. If it is a situation where it is a financial burden then contact the teacher in a timely manner before school starts and arrangements can be made to help you. Don't send your child to school to be successful without the necessary tools they need. It can also make them a target of ridicule from their peers. Remember to support the teachers and give them what they want, not what you think your child's supplies should be for their class.

Upon receiving an email, phone call, or note in the mail from one of your child's teachers, please respond as soon as possible. Ignoring a situation will only serve to exasperate it. Perhaps responding quickly will allow a resolution to a small problem before it escalates into a major incident. Teachers should contact parents with positive news as well, but usually the communication is about an issue. Respond to the teacher and hopefully the problem can be resolved quickly. You are paying attention to the teachers' concerns along with your child's and everyone can work together for a positive outcome.

As a parent you have certain responsibilities in providing daily needs for your child. Remember that the middle school child is hormonal and extremely irritable at times. This makes it difficult for the teacher to teach as well as the child to learn. However, sending your child to school day after day without them getting enough rest is counterproductive to whatever the teachers are trying to accomplish. I know you can't force your child to go to sleep but you can encourage them to get ready for bed at the same time every night. Set boundaries in hours spent watching television, playing computer games, being on social media or talking on their cell phone. Just because a child goes in their room it doesn't mean they are going to go to sleep at a reasonable hour. You only have to deal with them being irritable getting up in the morning. Teachers have to deal with their moodiness and exhaustion all day. I can't begin to tell you how many students have difficulty staying awake and focused in school, due to lack of sleep. This definitely drives teachers crazy because it's time taken away from instruction in waking the student up, and it disrupts the classroom as well as taking more time to maybe repeat what was just taught. Besides, no one wants to wake anyone up that needs or wants to sleep. It is the parent's responsibility to set boundaries when it comes to bedtime and follow through. Do not assume for a minute that just because you tell your middle schooler to go to bed at 10:00 they actually will go to sleep then.

Along the same lines, do not send your child to school sick. How do you feel when your coworker is in a meeting coughing and sneezing all over the place? Chances are if they are sick when they wake they will be sick when they get to school. Providing childcare is not always easy but exposing teachers and other students to illness is not acceptable either. Teachers are then susceptible to carrying the germs home to their family. Odds are if you keep your child home when they first get sick they will be out of school for a shorter period of time. Parents who send their sick child to school are doing a disservice to all.

Delaying school or closing schools for inclement weather has nothing to do with teachers. School administrators make these decisions. Parents have been known to blame teachers for things that occur in school when they are not within the teachers' control or realm of responsibilities. Complaining to a teacher about things they have no control over is definitely counterproductive. However it does occur and this makes the teacher's job more difficult.

Birthdays are a wonderful, special day for the person who is celebrating; however; bringing in treats without contacting the teacher ahead of time is not the proper thing to do. More upsetting is when parents send in birthday treats where the teacher is expected to find a knife to cut the cake, provide plates, plastic ware or drinks. This is totally unacceptable. That is not a teacher's job. You need to check with the school and find out the protocol for bringing in snacks. A final note on snacks is the teacher is responsible for food allergies for all students and needs to be very careful with foods sent in to school.

We all have extremely busy lives but it is important to be punctual to all school appointments. Teachers have limited time to meet with parents during the day so if you schedule a meeting be on time. First, this is the right thing to do and second it shows that what is occurring in your child's school day is important to you. If for some reason you can't make the appointment give the teacher the courtesy of a call prior to the meeting stating that you will be unable to make your appointment. Arriving late or not at all is disrespectful to the teacher.

The least we can do as parents is help to make teachers' jobs easier. They have a difficult job to begin with and any parental support is most welcomed. Teachers take care of your child all day long. They deal with hyperactive children, kids that can't focus, children with disabilities and numerous other issues. The last thing a parent should be doing is always being on the defensive or blaming the teacher. I am not saying the teachers are always right but at least hear them out, then make a calm judgment on what you've heard. Most importantly you and the teacher are on the same team. The winning one, that is in your child's best interest. The goal is to help your child, with their teacher's support, to provide a safe, successful learning environment.

Lastly, it is an understandable truth that teachers who know they have the support and cooperation of the parent tend to interact with the child more, which leads to a better relationship with them, which leads to a better atmosphere for them to learn.

10

Behavioral Issues

Once your child graduates from elementary school to middle school, there are behaviors that emerge and you ask yourself what happened to your quiet, well-mannered child. Parents would tell me that they are seeing negative behavioral changes at home and wondered if I witnessed the same behavior in my class. Most of the time, the parent received calls and or emails from me telling them their child was extremely talkative or exhibiting disruptive behavior. First their embarrassment was evident and then they apologized for their child being disruptive. Next, the comment was that their child never acted out in elementary school. Well, times they are a-changing. A whole new world has opened up to your middle schooler. New school, new friends, new experiences, and with that unfortunately comes some possibly negative behaviors.

Your neither fish nor fowl child may have difficulty understanding exactly where they fit in and with whom they want to be aligned. They no longer are the dependent elementary children but aren't quite an independent adult yet. They are somewhere in between. You will find they want to be less dependent and are upset that they don't have all the independence they feel that they should have. Unfortunately, the majority of middle school children still need money, require transportation to events, friends, store, etc. The difficulty lies in the fact that they want this independence and may not demonstrate the behavior to be as independent at they want. Let's not forget that their hormones are controlling their brains and peer pressure is affecting possible positive decision-making.

What's a parent to do during this transforming time? How does one live with a middle schooler's mood swings? You shouldn't blame your child for their irrational behavior, but you need to understand and try to put yourself in their shoes. You did go through this rough patch whether you want to remember or admit it. I feel very strongly that each age brings its own issues, problems and solutions. As mentioned numerous times in this book, your child may not want to talk or share with you the things that are going on in their lives; we need to find a way to have then open up. Sometimes empathy goes a long way. Ask them if you can help. They will probably say no, but that doesn't mean you should stop asking or trying ways to encourage them to share what is going on in their life.

Remember that fitting in with their peers is key to their happiness at this time. The problem is that it is a very fluid situation, which may change daily. Unfortunately, sometimes it is only a person not responding in the manner they had hoped for to ruin their entire day and put them in a bad mood where negative behaviors may appear.

Remember the term, "class clown?" It's still live and well. A good friend of mine who was starting to pull her hair out would say to me, "My son didn't say anything in elementary school, and now he doesn't stop talking in classes and says everyone thinks that whatever he says is funny." She would tell me she doesn't even recognize her own child and the school's number is on her speed dial. She would also report that she and some of her son's teachers emailed so much that they became friends.

What do I mean by negative behaviors? Well as you know there is a wide range of behaviors that a person can exhibit. As a teacher, the definition for me of negative behaviors in a classroom are those that in any way disrupt a teacher from instructing the rest of the class. It could be as minor as constant talking to annoying other students to cursing to yelling to throwing things or fighting, just to mention a few.

That's another issue, fighting. For some reason middle school kids seem to rather solve problems by starting fights than by verbally working things out. When the behaviors become more serious, so do the consequences. The classroom teacher can handle some issues while others have to involve the administration. As a parent you should always be aware of any behavioral issues.

Sometimes you will see evidence of changes in your child's behaviors at home. It is difficult for the adolescent to change gears when it comes to their inappropriate behavior. For instance, as an adult you know you need to control your anger at work and you can't say aloud everything that enters your head mainly because you want to keep your job. A middle schooler seems to have no filter at times and whatever enters their mind comes right out of their mouth. I was known to tell kids all the time that the reason they had two ears and only one mouth was that they were supposed to listen more and speak less, which most of the time was a waste of my breath.

So how should a parent deal with their child when they exhibit behaviors that are not acceptable? You can always punish your child in a way that you feel is appropriate, but please remember that the punishment needs to fit the crime. Or you can tell them that the behavior is unacceptable and explain why while presenting them with an alternative way to handle the situation that has them upset.

My father was a traveling salesman and most weeks he was away until the weekend. One of my mother's favorite things to tell my brothers and me was that she was going to tell him what we did and he would assign the punishment when he came home. However, most times my father chose not to be the disciplinarian and we forgot what we did that got my mother so upset. So, it's important to deal with the unacceptable behavior sooner than later.

Adolescents at times have difficulty seeing things from other peoples' perspective, so if you can explain to them how their behavior either hurt someone or was inappropriate they may choose a different, more positive reaction the next time.

You put your rather innocent, sweet, kind child on the bus to middle school one day and a know it all, grown up, perhaps a little nasty child gets off the bus. What really happens in middle school to cause these behavioral changes? The answer is as simple as "other kids."

In the 1980s the phrase "latchkey kid" became prevalent. Basically, it referred to kids who carried their house key since their parents were working and no one was home when they came home after school. The reason I mention this is because today a large number of middle school children spend a lot of time alone and they need to fend for themselves. In caring for himself or herself they may be worldlier or "street smart" since there is no one home to help or support them sometimes until late in the evening. If a middle schooler has come from a home where there are others to take care of them, they may not have been exposed to some challenges that other kids have experienced.

11

Importance of Extra Curricular Activities

There's a proverb that says, "All work and no play makes Jack a dull boy." I'm sure every adult can relate to this saying and understands that it's not good to work all the time. People get bored, unhappy and even resentful around others. This feeling is no different for children. Your child is in school for a minimum of six hours a day and then may have hours of homework to complete. Everyone needs an outlet from his or her daily grind.

Extracurricular activities are an integral part of the middle school experience. Not only is it important for your child to experience new endeavors, it's an opportunity for them to meet and develop new friendships outside their circle of friends.

As a parent you should encourage your child to attend a meeting about a club or sport they may be interested in and learn about the activity to see if they want to join. All activities are posted around the building as well as mentioned in morning or afternoon announcements. I had the opportunity to be the advisor for the National Junior Honor Society as well as SADD (Students Against Drunken Driving), which later changed to Students Against Destructive Decisions. Running these clubs allowed me the opportunity to meet students who were not in my classes and interact with them on a non academic level and really get to know them as the young, wonderful people they were without having to assign them a grade.

So, the real question is are these extracurricular activities going to enrich your child's life? Yes, they most definitely will. Your child will be learning new things like to play chess, student council, debate club or writing for the school newspaper or yearbook. Today everyone loves taking pictures with their phone. And being allowed to take pictures of their friends in the halls and classes for the yearbook is a lot of fun. That's the word that sums up the value of these activities, having FUN.

Another advantage of extracurricular activities is it gives your child an opportunity to excel in a non-academic environment. Sports are an excellent avenue for a young adult to learn about being a team player and being part of a team. Physical exercise is a great way for a person to de-stress and get fit at the same time. There are many sports available during the school year. Middle school is a great time for a young person to experience playing different sports and finding their niche.

Another saying is "kids who do sports don't do drugs." In my opinion, the more activities a young person gets involved in, the less time they have to get in any type of trouble. Remember, middle school kids are impressionable and the fuller their lives are in organized events, the happier they will be. If your child is not interested in athletic activities there are numerous clubs and activities that are available at any middle school. Sometimes, a student will go to hear about a new club at the request of a friend and find him or herself interested in joining even though they weren't even considering it. Some clubs are short term while others last an entire school year. Your child can join as many extracurricular activities as their schedule–and yours–allows.

There are extracurricular activities that your child can become involved in that are not associated with their school. For instance, there are sports that are run by the town, which allow your child to meet other kids that may not necessarily attend their school. You as parent may involve your child in private tennis, golf, or perhaps music lessons. Your child may be attending an after school program where they can work on their homework and spend time with other kids their age.

The goal here is not to let your child sit home alone without parental supervision. Middle school kids when left to their own devices do not always make the best choices.

Having been a single, working mom, I know the challenges can be overwhelming even to set up transportation to and from these events. Most schools provide late buses and there is the possibility of car-pooling. In addition to the traveling to and from these events there may be financial concerns. There are sports programs that provide assistance through scholarships. There is definitely help for any parent who needs some direction or assistance in arranging some of these activities. Do not get discouraged and feel free to reach out to the guidance counselors in your school since they can provide a wealth of information. Talk to other parents and ask for help when you need it. I know that is easier said than done because I personally had a difficult time asking others to give me a hand, but I would be the first to help others. So, I finally gave in and found that other parents had the same problems and issues. We watched each other's kids, arranged transportation schedules, and were sounding boards for each other.

Just a word to the wise: be careful in allowing your kids to over extend themselves by joining too many activities. Remember they have a lot of homework and require lots of sleep, so try to find the right balance and your middle school student will have a full but manageable life.

12

Understanding Learning Styles

If you've ever thought about how you learn something new, you would realize that you have a preferred way of learning. Before cell phones, Google maps and GPS if someone would tell me directions, I would get a glazed look on my face. When they were finished, in a very sweet tone, I would say, "Can you write that out for me, please?" When I would just listen somewhere my brain was saying I would never get to my destination but when I could visually read the directions my brain was saying I could find this place.

Some people have one dominant learning style [12] while others may utilize different styles depending on what the situation is requiring them to process. Learning styles do not have to be fixed in the sense you can only learn by one technique or couldn't benefit from a combination of styles. What we can agree on is, not everyone learns the same way.

As a reading teacher I always felt it was my job to help students understand how they could best learn. As an adjunct professor I became aware very early in a semester that college freshman still did not know their preferred learning style or really what the term meant. They would tell me they didn't like certain professors and when I would question them as to why, the general consensus was they had difficulty understanding the professor's way of teaching. Clearly stated, if an instructor's method of teaching doesn't coordinate with a student's dominant or preferred learning style minimal learning may take place.

If you were to research learning styles you will probably find seven or more that are identified. For our purposes there are four main styles. The other styles deal with spatial learning, mathematics and interpersonal skills. In understanding your dominant learning style the optimum result would be improving the speed and quality in your learning.

Visual Learning Style incorporates teaching that uses pictures, images and an understanding of spatial relationships. This style is prominent in elementary school. Think about how a classroom is decorated. There are all types of visuals in the room from charts to pictures to definitions to diagrams. English language learners, (ELL), benefit from this style of instruction.

The majority of middle school classrooms are not highly decorated since some teachers move from class to class and others feel that it looks too elementary if there are a lot of pictures, posters, etc. So middle school students do not have as much visual stimuli around them. If the room has posters or definitions or charts on the wall, they are very content specific just for that course. If your child learns best from visual cues, they probably will not be seeing as many as they were used to in their elementary school. Middle and high school teachers have a lot of content to cover and feel pressured to prepare students for state tests, so there is a lot of talking occurring without as much visual stimuli. For the visual learner this is a change for them and possibly a disruption in their learning until they are able to prepare for another learning style.

Auditory Learning Style focuses on listening intently to what is being discussed. This style is preferred for musicians, learning and discriminating between sounds. The difficulty with this strategy is that you need to be focusing 100%, otherwise you may miss important information. Most lectures are purely auditory in nature that is why many students record lectures. If there are other distractions occurring, such as noise in or outside the classroom, listening becomes a more difficult task. It would never fail when I needed to talk about a new topic the lawn movers or weed whackers were going full steam outside. In middle school kids are always tired and sitting still and listening becomes an overwhelming task. So needless to say, if they're not listening intently, they are bound to not hear important information. Now, some kids do listen well but it's sometimes difficult to differentiate the important information from extraneous material.

Kinesthetic Learning Style is usually the most popular style because everyone learns from doing. Kinesthetic involves a hands-on approach to learning. This style is generally used for leaning with students that are energetic and think best while they're moving. You are doing instead of just listening or watching someone else perform a task. As a teacher, evidence that a student learned a concept, theory, or geometry proof was to have them explain it to someone else. This indicated that they mastered what was being taught.

The Kinesthetic Style is how the majority of us learn. The problem is not every teacher has the time, ability, or materials available to provide this type of instruction. In middle school the more popular courses are those where the kids can do hands-on activities. Doing science experiments, cooking in home economics, creating a power point in computer lab is a lot more interesting and fun than just sitting in a class listening to an instructor talk. So, how can one utilize tactile strategies? With parents' assistance and support activities this can be developed at home. Remember, in school most teachers would love to give every student individualized instruction; however our public school system is not equipped for that.

The Tactile Learning Style is for students who "often like to draw or doodle to remember." This modality is often selected by students who, "do best when they take notes either during a lecture or when reading something new or difficult."

All four of these Learning Styles are effective teaching methods. Most students use all of them or a combination depending upon the situation. However, it is important for every student to gain an understanding of their preferred learning style and how they; learn new information. If a teacher only talks and doesn't provide any visuals and that student is not an auditory learner, it is imperative for them to speak up and possibly ask if the teacher can give a visual example. Every student is responsible for his or her own learning. They have to be proactive, which means to ask questions, interact with the teacher and other students, as well as when reading highlight important details and question as they read.

Learning styles can change for a student depending on their needs as well as the instruction being provided. For example, if your child comes home from middle school and tells you they don't like a subject or a teacher, first ask what the problem is that they are experiencing. It could be as simple as them not understanding the way the teacher provides instruction or presents information.

Think about your own experiences. If you have difficulty understanding what is going on you probably experience feelings of frustration and possibly some anxiety. In elementary school your child had one teacher providing all instruction and was aware of each student's strengths and weaknesses. In middle school the teacher spends approximately forty minutes a day with your child and is unable to develop the same relationship. Additionally, as kids get older more of the learning responsibility rests on the student. There are clashes between teaching styles and learning styles and if these are not addressed grades drop, inappropriate behaviors may surface, as well as negative feelings towards the course and ultimately the teacher. The best way to address this is to schedule an appointment to meet with the specific teacher and address all your concerns. This may be an appropriate meeting for your child to attend. Your child is the one who can explain what they are feeling and experiencing with the teacher. Communication is the key in resolving this problem. As your child gets older they will learn to utilize the different learning styles to accommodate their learning style preference.

As a general rule, most of us benefit the most from the kinesthetic approach to learning because when we are able to have a hands-on experience we seem to process the information better and therefore retain it. Some of us are better listeners than others so we are tuned in the Auditory Learning Style. Visual learners are able to use visual aids to remember and retain information. Tactile learners are also kinesthetic learners who prefer to be actively engaged in their learning. "Most children that are kinesthetic learners become more tactile in the first grade." [13] There is not one better style than another: it is purely a personal preference, and the important thing is to be aware that there are learning styles to help your child be successful in school.

13

Coping Strategies

This book could have all been about coping strategies to aid parents in living with a middle school child. Elementary age kids and high schoolers have their own issues, problems and concerns but the middle school child is unique. Some days you think to yourself where did I go wrong or who does this child really belong to, because it's not mine. When I deal with people, I always listen and try to be empathetic and I put myself as best as I can in their shoes. That's what you have to do with your middle school child even if they appear alien to you at times. Keep telling yourself that it's those hormones that have taken over their mind and body.

I'm not telling you how to parent your child, just some helpful strategies to guide them through these tumultuous years. The challenge with the middle school child is their issues may not just be academic but expand into dealing with friends, especially peer pressure, wearing inappropriate clothing, moodiness, being argumentative, and laziness. Don't get me wrong; your middle school child is not a monster, just a confused adolescent who is trying to find their way in this world. Unfortunately it is a different world than we grew up in at the same age.

Middle school is a very challenging and turbulent time for both the parent and the child but it doesn't have to be if both parties are prepared.

The first step is a smooth transition from elementary to middle school. The more familiar your child is with their new school the more comfortable they will feel about attending middle school. It would be advantageous to take your child to any program for incoming students where they have an opportunity to tour the school, meet the staff, meet other students and have an opportunity to ask questions. At the end of every school year we would talk to the sixth grade population and ask them what their biggest concerns and fears were about going to middle school. Every year the issues were the same. Not in any particular order, they were: finding their classes, opening their locker, being accepted and liked by other students and just fitting in with their peers.

Most important for a parent is, to stay involved in your child's life. As much as your child may push you away, stay connected with them. Do whatever it takes to keep lines of communication open even though they may want to push you away because they want to figure out things by themselves. Stay in touch with their teachers. Most teachers post a lot of information on the school's website as well as their email address for you to easily contact them. Communication is the key. The earlier a problem or situation is addressed the better it is for all parties involved. There is the possibility that your child will not readily open up about a situation until they are ready, and then things may have escalated into a larger issue. So, always keep a vigilant eye on any behavioral changes, sleep pattern changes, eating irregularities and any behavior that is not normal for your child. All these could be signs that your child is having difficulties in school.

So the real question, is how can we help our children to be successful in these transition years in middle school. I have identified some tips to assist you as a parent to help your child deal with harder work, more classes and teachers that all have different expectations as well as personalities.

If I had to identify one element to success in middle school, it would be organizational skills. I can't emphasize enough the importance of helping your child to develop an organized system for keeping track of assignments, home-work, notes and important papers. Some schools provide free planners or ones that can be purchased at a reasonable price to encourage organization. You can also buy your own for your child to use on a daily basis. Depending on a teacher's list of necessary materials for their class, I always recommended to parents to buy individual folders for each class and not one big binder for all subjects. Within a few weeks, that binder becomes fifty pounds of an unorganized mess.

Try to designate a time weekly to clean out the folders. Maybe the weekend when there is some down time or Sunday night in preparation for the upcoming week. You may have to sit down with your child at first to help them and then slowly let them be responsible for keeping their papers in an organized manner. Some people are naturally organized while others are missing the organizational gene and need to be shown more than once how to master this task. Your help and support at this time will definitely pay off in the long run.

In addition to helping your child with their organizational skills, it is important to teach them about time management.

The most important thing is to help your child estimate the time it will take them to complete homework, a project, prepare for a test, or any assigned work. I used to joke with my daughter that next to the word procrastinator in the dictionary was her picture because she never allowed enough time for her assignments and would be up late at night completing her work. Her underestimation of the time needed to complete assignments was a definite stress catalyst. In learning how to deal with time management the pressures your child will experience will be minimized.

In addition to managing how long assignments will take, it is important to provide your child with a designated area for them to work that is well lit, quiet and conducive to completing their work. At the beginning of middle school, a specific time should be set up for your child to do their homework. Some kids like to start their homework as soon as they get home from school, while others want to relax, and some kids like to do their assignments after dinner. Sometimes when your child gets more involved with school activities, they have less free time and fitting in schoolwork becomes a bigger problem. As long as you feel your child can balance schoolwork, and extracurricular activities as well as any other responsibilities they make have at home they will have a most successful time in middle school.

Another strategy that needs to be addressed is note taking. Kids need to be taught how to evaluate, organize and summarize information. Kids are not taught how to take notes the way we were when we went to school. I know you remember taking notes using Roman Numerals. If you give a middle school student a highlighter and tell them to use it to highlight important information in their textbook, the entire page will be yellow. It is a learned task to figure out what is considered important as compared to extraneous information. Then there is the daunting task of taking that important material and making notes from what was read. You may not feel very comfortable in helping your child to take notes, but you can Google how to take notes and a variety of methods will appear. You can help your child to identify the note taking method that works best for them.

Teachers will write notes and have students copy them but when a child enters middle school they are now expected to take notes on what they hear and read.

There is a simple strategy called the SQ3R. This stands for Survey, Question, Read, Recite and Review. This strategy helps the student to think about the material in the textbook they are reading while they are reading it. Once the notes are taken they can be used later for studying. This method can be used during middle school through college.

Along with great organizational skills, it is necessary to provide your child with structure and routine at home. Remember, both you and your child are adjusting to many changes. You will need to stay connected with your child's schedule and activities. There may also need to be adjustments made to your personal schedule to accommodate extracurricular activities, homework, projects and extra studying time. Your work schedule may need to be adjusted as well as extra planning for activities or perhaps carpooling arrangements. A giant calendar or lots of post-its work well as reminders and a way to communicate. Your child needs to have a place to leave important school papers that need to be signed or any notes from teachers. As time goes on your child can have more responsibility in schedule planning but in the beginning of the school year, you will need to do most of the scheduling.

Routines are important. Everyone does well with structure whether they want to admit it or not. If you expect your child to have household chores then these need to be planned into the weekly schedule. A new school year always brings challenges but being organized with set schedules and routines will aid in a smooth transition.

As previously mentioned, staying involved in your child's life will only strengthen and enhance your relationship with them during some of the most trying years of their life as well as yours.

Your child may experience some uneasiness in communicating with their teachers. Speaking to their friends is a lot different from them expressing feelings, concerns or apprehension about work or issues in the classroom with a teacher. If your child is shy or has had difficulty with expressing their feelings in the past, write an email to their teachers and explain the best way for them to communicate with your child. You can even give the teacher a heads up that your child would Ike to speak to them. Like anything else, after doing it the first couple of times, it becomes easier and your child will gain more confidence in their ability to communicate with adults.

Parent conferences taught me, as the saying goes, "tricks of the trade." Listening to other parents share their concerns and anxieties helped me to become more sensitive and aware of ways for all to survive the middle school years. The word that you will learn a new definition for is drama. A blog from a teacher, Mrs. Mondragon states, "These years are a hormonal rollercoaster." [14] She recommends that parents educate themselves by reading about the stress kids feel in middle school about fitting in and puberty. She recommends reading the book <u>Queen Bees and Wannabees</u> by Rosalind Wiseman. The book is for parents of daughters, nieces or granddaughters attending middle school.

14

Life After Middle School

You will survive these challenging years and come out on the other side stronger, wiser, maybe with a little more gray hair, but in time look at those challenging years and be able to smile knowing your child is entering adulthood. High school will bring other experiences and opportunities for you and your young adult. There may be more uncertainty and anxiety with the high school years but remember there are other adults to support you and your child through the next four years of their educational career. There are teachers, guidance counselors, other school professionals as well as administrators to guide you through these wonderful and exciting years. In addition you can always reach out to other parents and friends for support.

As middle school ends and the high school years begin you will notice distinctive changes in your child. Maturity is setting in along with hormones leveling off and you will be able to start having intelligent conversations with your young adult. There will be a transformation before your eyes.

Your once self-centered at times child is now metamorphosing into the beginning stages of adulthood. You will be able to reason with them and find that they are more helpful, compassionate and all around easier to live with at home. They are slowly becoming a responsible person with logical thoughts and reasoning ability. They will begin to think about future planning instead of just immediate gratification and have a better understanding of actions and consequences.

Your "neither fish nor fowl," child will start becoming a productive member of society. Don't think that your high school student will not test your limits or bring different problems into their and your daily life, but being able to have a discussion where they actually listen and participate is definitely a step towards maturity.

When our children are little, we seem to be able to solve their problems easily. Older kids tend to have problems that require more effort on everyone's part to resolve them. As my children got older I realized that the problems are just age appropriate and that life for all of us is a learning process. None of us get it right all the time. We should learn from our mistakes and grow wiser and stronger in spite of them.

A good friend called me hysterically a few days before the end of the school year. It was the evening of the eighth grade Moving up Ceremony and she was upset that her "baby" was headed to high school in the fall. Although she was relieved that middle school was coming to an end, she coincidentally, received a call from her son's principal. She thought it had to be a mistake. Apparently, her son was aware of a bullying situation at school. The principal was calling to obtain any information concerning the incident. The young man had information but was sworn to secrecy by the girl involved.

Middle school as well as high school students definitely put their bonds of friendship first and foremost. It did become a teachable moment and it became readily apparent to my friend's son that he was not as grown up as he thought and that he didn't handle the situation well.

So, what can you really look forward to in the upcoming high school years? Well, you will still be butting heads at times with your child, and the issue of trust may come up more than once because remember they are still evolving and testing limits. Now they are becoming more independent and want to do everything on their own. The problem is, they still live in your home and need to follow your rules. High school students have busier schedules with perhaps more demands on their time. For example, longer sports time commitments, more schoolwork, more extracurricular activities, part-time jobs and dating. Now you're thinking middle school was simpler, but it is all part of growing up and becoming an adult. We all went through it and survived, if maybe only by the skin of our teeth.

As a parent you need to step back a little and let them experience life, but be close enough to catch them when they fall or just need some direction or advice. One of the hardest things for a parent is to stand by even when you know your child might get hurt. The important thing is to continue to communicate with them, stay involved in their life, and be there to hold them and comfort them when they make the wrong decision or take a chance and fail.

15

Survival Tips For Living With a Middle School Aged Child

1. Most importantly you love your child. No matter what they may do or how crazy they make you feel, you are the one they can rely on; however, it's okay to feel you don't like the person they are at this present time.

2. Focus on all the positive things your child has done in their lives and all the happiness they have brought to your life before entering middle school.

3. Spend time on the weekends and holidays engaging in fun, family activities.

4. Incorporate some one-on-one time with your child at home. Some suggestions are: cooking together, building or repairing something, painting, watching movies, playing one of their favorite video games. Get to know your child and what interests them at this present time in their life.

5. Find some solace that you were once their age, and had no common sense and your parents still let you live in their home.

6. Remember crazy high school years are around the corner with new challenges, fears and concerns. The prospect of having a real conversation with your child is in arm's reach.

7. Always keep lines of communication open. Let your child know that you understand how truly confusing, challenging and possibly difficult their life can seem right now.

8. Try to be nonjudgmental when you do engage in discussions. Let your child talk and really listen to what they are saying because it is important to them. Also, support them but be careful not to enable them. They need to problem solve and find solutions for themselves.

9. With hectic schedules, if possible, find avenues of release for yourself such as meditation, an adult education course (something fun), talking walks, or just doing something that makes "you" happy. These activities can help you approach life in a more positive manner. In taking time for yourself, your time with your child will be less stressful.

10. Most importantly find humor in the issues you are dealing with and you might find yourself laughing.

16

The Condition of Middle Schools Today

Before I can conclude this book, I feel very strongly that it would be negligent of me not to impart to you the state of our middle schools today. Just pick up any newspaper or turn on the television and you're well aware of today's educational system.

With some schools reporting all-time highs in weapon confiscations, while others are making it harder by initiating a school policy to suspend unruly and aggressive students. It's no wonder that we're filled with angst in our every waking moment. What used to be, "it's not in my town," has become much too commonplace for comfort. As parents our job is to educate our children and ourselves by getting involved and speaking out to authority. It's all about awareness.

More as a summary than a separate chapter I need to stress the importance of your involvement as a parent. At times, middle school can be a battlefield. You need to protect your child from the daily events they encounter in their classes.

A veteran math middle school teacher wrote an article in the New York Post and stated that, "I've never seen such a disregard for the rules —and human decency—as I'm see-ing now."

The best way for you to help your child through these un-settling years is to be completely involved in their day-to-day lives. In order to do this you need to keep lines of communi-cation open with your child, teachers, and school. It may be difficult since adolescents would rather talk to their friends instead of their parent.

The problem today in most schools, especially at the mid-dle school level is the students are in control and not the teachers. The teachers have limited say in what happens to a student who is disrespectful or out of control.

The administration gets sanctioned for having too many students suspended in a specific time period. Therefore, in certain situations, their hands are driven more by the ad-ministrative politics than what is good for the students. This means that students do not receive an appropriate punish-ment for their inappropriate behavior. A student can cause a major disruption in class and return the following day to the same class causing more problems.

Your child is witnessing the negative behavior, but more importantly sees the student returning to class and sits in the class where the inappropriate behavior continues. Middle school kids will share with each other the fact that there were no consequences for their outburst and that they can do what-ever they want without repercussions. What message is this sending to your child? So your child is starting to question, "Why do I have to behave?"

Unfortunately, the student getting the attention is the one that is not behaving instead of the A student who never causes a problem and does all their work. Teachers spend the majority of class time dealing with behavioral issues and resolving problems between students. Your child needs to be able to express their concerns and frustrations that they are feeling. They may be reluctant to open up because they don't want to be considered a tattletale or get anyone in trouble. They need to be able to tell you what occurs during their day without you being judgmental or running to call the school. Your primary concern is the safety and well being of your child.

Once your child has shared events that have occurred, together you and your child can discuss a plan of action. Your child can be present when you discuss issues with their teacher or you can tell them what took place after your meeting. The occasion may arise where you will be dealing with the administration and your child may not be invited to attend. Regardless of how the problem is handled, your child is the one who attends school and should be told what they can expect in their classroom.

Aside from classroom issues, today's children are coping with very serious issues. Schools have been the scene of too much rancor leading to violence. Keeping your child safe is the school's primary job, but not every school is prepared for unforeseen calamities. Every parent should be aware of the school's plan for intruders, lock down procedures, and safety drills. The more informed you are, the more comfortable your child can feel. Be there to answer their questions and reassure them as best as you can. There are professionals who can assist in helping you and your child cope with these horrendous events that we all are confronted with in today's society.

We can deal with things that are within our control. The problem is not being able to deal with the things out of our control. Middle school can and should be a time of growth and exploration for you child but in a safe environment.

Adolescence is the beginning of your child's independence. This brings many challenges physically, emotionally, socially, and perhaps spiritually. Knowing right from wrong is a daily challenge for some. Friendships are paramount in their lives. Children need their parents more now than before. The problem is, your child wants you less in their life.

Surviving the middle school years unscathed for your child and yourself is possible. Parental involvement and communication is the key. Remember just because your child pushes you away, they are still waiting for you to be there for them.

Helpful Websites

http://sweetsearch.com/sweetsites/categories/middle-school/students
search engine from Dulcenia Media for help with school work

readwritethink.org
resources for parents to help with their child's literacy

http://www.pta.org
parent-teacher association web page with information for parents

shmoop.com
collection of study guides created by teachers & educators to help kids with homework and test preparation

brainpop.com
site for exploring school topics to satisfy your child's curiosity

merriam-webster.com
comprehensive dictionary

mathplayground.com
kids can play games, solve logic problems and watch math videos

sophia.org
test taking strategies

safesearchkids.com
site powered by Google for safe filtered search results

britannica.com>kids
an online encyclopedia resource for kids in grades K-12

Homework Sites

khanacademy.org
a personalized learning resource for all ages

bj pinchbeck's homework helper
free homework resources for students and parents

hippocampus.org
site offers video, audio and written tutorials

factmonster.com
site covers the basics of a variety of topics for students ages eight to fourteen looking to find information quickly

coolmath.com
helpful math website with practice worksheets

grammerbook.com/sweetsites/categories/middle-school/students
a guidebook for students wanting to know the correct mechanics of writing

Helpful Websites for Parents of Children with Disabilities

add.org
Attention Deficit Disorder Association

www.ldresources.com
Learning Disability Resources

www.ncld.org
National Center for Learning Disabilities

References

1   In schools, strategies such as teaming…
    www.edglossary.org (teaming)
2   You should expect…
    parenttool.com
3   Many times your personal knowledge…
    www.usnews.com
4   The brain's most dramatic…
    Adolescent Angst : 5 Facts About the Teen Brain
    www.livescience.com
5   Dr. Benjamin Bloom…
    www.teachthought.com
6   Can I walk from here….
    The Great Alone, Kristen Hannah, St. Martin's Press, Center
    Point 2018 Large Print Thorndike, Maine
    pp. 87-88 ISBN: 978-1-68324-700-5
7   Students' middle school grades…
    getschooled.com
8   The middle school years…
    blog.ed.gov
9   Test Anxiety
    adaa.org
10 Giftedness may manifest…
    www.verywellfamily.com
    Most people fall in the range…
    Http://www.verywellfamily.com/what-is-a-gifted-child-
    1449130

11 There is more than one IQ test...
    Http://www.nagc.lrg
12 Learning Styles
    www.peralta.edu
13 Most children are kinesthetic learners...
    www.peralta.edu
14 These years are a hormonal roller coaster...
    mrs.mondragon.weebly.com
    Listening to other parents...
    Top Five Tips for Parents to Survive Middle School
    mrsmondragon.weebly.com
15 I've never seen such a disregard for the rules...
    https://nypost.com/2019/03/05my-students- know-they're-in-ch...nothing-I-can-do

Printed in the United States
By Bookmasters